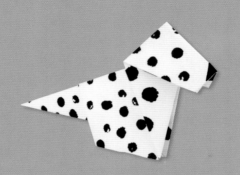

COLOURGAMI

COLOURGAMI

THE ART OF PAPER FOLDING
AND CREATIVE COLOURING

NICK ROBINSON

ARCTURUS

This edition published in 2017 by Arcturus Publishing Limited
26/27 Bickels Yard, 151–153 Bermondsey Street,
London SE1 3HA

ISBN: 978-1-78428-543-2
AD005534UK

Printed in China

CONTENTS

Introduction 6
Materials and tools 7
How to fold 8
Techniques 10
Bases 14
Decorating origami 16

Beginner projects 18
Crown 20
Cup 22
Whale 24
Bellflower 26
Buttonhole 30
Dog 32
Glider 34
Blinking eye 36
Snapper 38
Chair 40
Wolf 42
Fish profile 44

Advanced projects 48
Elephant head 50
Container 52
Duck 56
Monkey 58
Pajarita 62
Rabbit 64
Rocking penguin 66
Shubunkin 68
Tulip 72
Tropical fish 74
Space shuttle 78
Hen 80
High heels 84
Star 86
Ackworth dish 88
Angel 92

Acknowledgements 96

INTRODUCTION

In a time when our lives are immersed in technology such as mobile phones, computers and the internet, it's all too easy to lose touch with the simple pleasures of life. One of these is undoubtedly 'colouring in'. We all did it as children, but somehow it seems to be lost from our lives as we grow older. However, more and more adults are rediscovering the joys of using crayons and pencils to make simple (or complex) patterns on paper.

Origami is a Japanese word that means 'folding paper'. It is commonly used for the art or craft of making models from paper. Origami paper is available in many different colours and patterns, but here is a wonderful opportunity to create your own designs! Each of the fold guidelines is shown on the coloured templates provided for each project, so you can replicate the guidelines and colour in the facets any way you wish. The process of "colouring in" has been established as a wonderful way to relieve stress and use your creativity at the same time. Add to this the pleasure of folding origami models and you are guaranteed a wonderful, relaxing time working through this book.

So, a combination of folding and colouring really helps as a 'mindfulness mantra' by which we can focus our minds and forget our worries. Try to appreciate the various physical aspects of the process – the sounds made by folding paper, the feel of the paper as you make a crease. Stop every now and again and try to draw on ambient stimuli such as external sounds, scents and the weather. There are many simple pleasures in life that we often overlook.

Materials and tools

- Oil pastels and water-based paint, the latter requires the use of a small paint brush, which you should clean each time you use it, both before and after.

- Pencils and crayons are among the easiest media with which to decorate the paper, since we all have existing skills in this area, even if they are from long ago.

- Collage effects can be created by cutting out shapes to fit specific areas and gluing them to the paper. This does however make the paper thicker and so hard to fold neatly.

- For print effects use small sponges to apply your custom patterns to the paper.

How to fold

When folding and decorating, try to create a suitable environment – play relaxing music, find some 'quiet time', have all your materials to hand on a clean open space, arrange suitable lighting so you can see exactly what you are doing. The process will automatically help you to de-stress as you concentrate your mind on the task in hand.

Origami uses a simple series of symbols that tell you how and where to fold. Once you have learned these, the whole world of origami is opened up to you and you can even follow instructions that may be in a different language! The key to mastery is to fold slowly and carefully. Make each crease as accurately as you can by taking enough time to line up edges and points before making the crease. After creasing, re-fold along the lines to make the crease sharp and neat. If a step isn't working for you, try folding again with a fresh sheet. Sometimes, it's advisable to leave the model for a day or two and revisit it before you complete it.

The models in this book are arranged in a general order of complexity, so you are recommended to fold them in the order in which they are presented. All of the projects are designed with one side of the paper used for colouring in. In order to avoid having a white underside showing in your finished model, I advise you do what I have done and use origami paper sheets that already have a plain colour on one side (there are some provided with this book). The instructions for each project will make it clear which is your coloured side and which is your plain side. Although, there is one project (Blinking Eye) that you will need to colour on both sides.

For every project, you will find coloured templates that you can follow. Before you attempt to fold your finished coloured sheet, I recommend practising folding the model several times using plain paper in order to master the folding sequence. Once you are confident about folding a model, you can use your coloured sheet and make the final product.

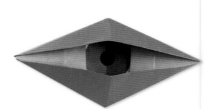

If you wish to colour the design in your own, unique way, first fold a blank sheet to see what the finished model will look like. This will allow you to decide how you want to decorate each exposed area. Then you can mark up the folded model indicating which colours you want to put where, unfold it and use it as your own template for making a clean, finished version.

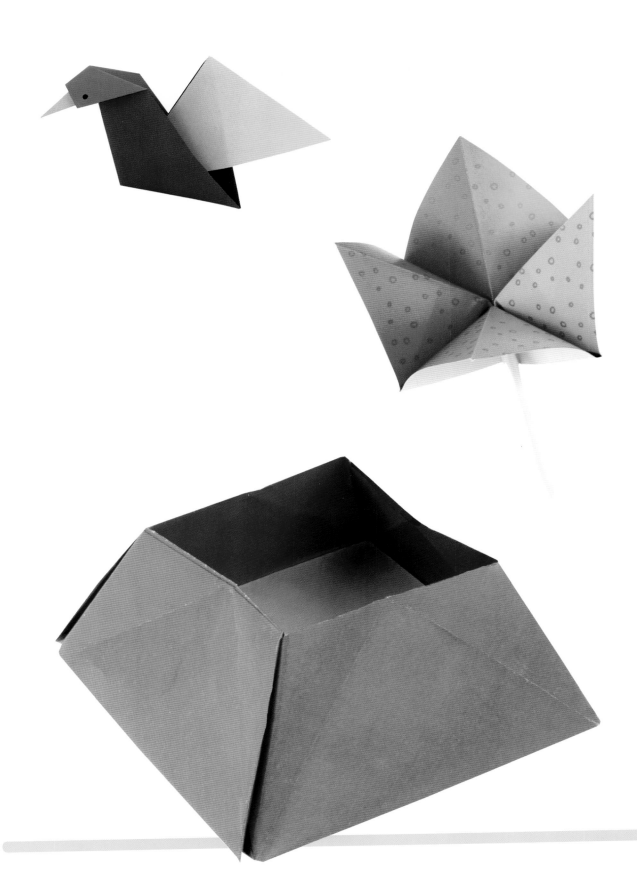

Techniques

The most important techniques to learn are the types of folds you will be expected to make. For each of the designs, the step-by-step instructions will include symbols that indicate which folding technique you should use. The symbols are easy to learn.

Over the past fifty years, origami instructions (often called diagrams) have been refined and expanded, but they still use a core set of folding symbols. These are universally recognized and give enough information for you to follow diagrams regardless of the language that may be used. After a while, they become second nature to you and you will easily be able to follow them. They are also important if you design your own models and wish to share them.

Valley fold

The most basic of all folds – a corner or edge is lined up with another corner or edge. The paper should form a "V" shape with the crease at the bottom. The name comes from the finished shape which resembles a valley, or trough.

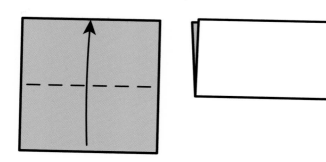

Valley and unfold
Make the valley fold, then unfold it, leaving a crease.

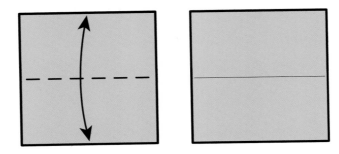

Mountain fold
The opposite of a valley fold, here the paper is folded behind. If you find it easier, you can turn the paper over, make a valley fold, then turn it back over again. Sometimes, it's simplest just to fold underneath.

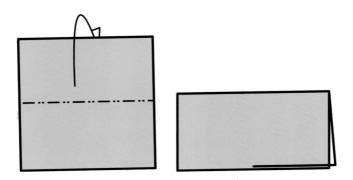

Repeat arrow

This arror (top) shows you how many times a step is to be repeated, on the opposite side, or maybe on all four sides.

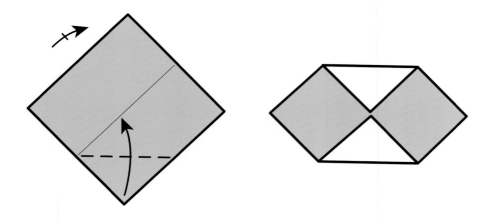

Pleat

A valley and mountain fold can be combined to form a pleat.

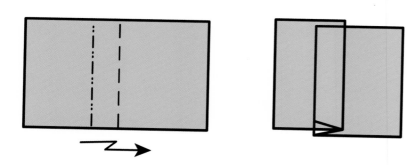

Turn the paper over

Flip the paper over from side to side, like tossing a pancake!

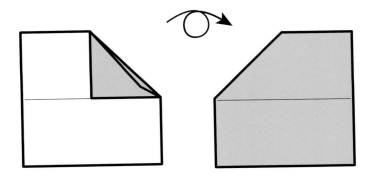

Turn the paper round

Rotate the paper, usually either 90 or 180 degrees.

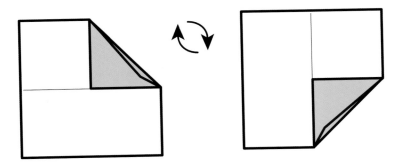

Bases

Some sequences of initial folds are used regularly and are called "bases". Here are some quick instructions for the bases used in this book.

Kite base

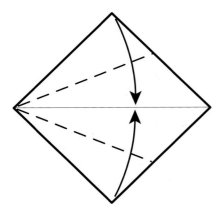

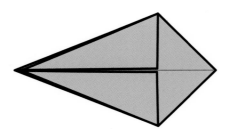

Take a square sheet of paper and position it like a diamond shape. Make a horizontal fold along the centre and unfold.

Next fold top left and bottom left edges to align with the central crease.

Preliminary base

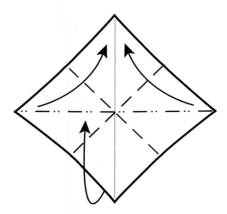

Take a square sheet of paper and position it like a diamond shape. Make a horizontal mountain fold along the centre by folding the top point behind to meet the bottom point and unfold.

Next, fold the paper in half, diagonally, and unfold. Do this in both directions to form an X shaped crease.

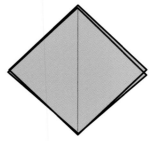

Now fold the bottom point up to meet the top corner and, while doing so, make mountain folds along your horizontal crease.

Waterbomb base

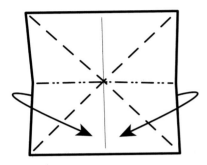

Take a square sheet of paper, fold the paper in half, vertically, and unfold. Make a horizontal mountain fold along the centre by folding the top half behind and unfold.

Next, fold the paper in half, diagonally, and unfold. Do this in both directions to form an X shaped crease.

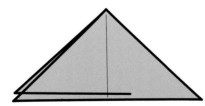

Now fold the paper in half from top to bottom and, while doing so, make valley folds along your horizontal crease.

Windmill/Multiform base

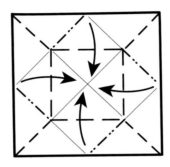

Take a square sheet of paper and fold it diagonally, and unfold, in both directions to fold an X shaped crease across the centre. Then fold each corner behind, to the centre, and unfold. Now fold each edge of the square to along with the centre and unfold.

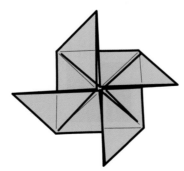

Using these creases, fold your edges back into the centre, but make sure to carefully fold out the corners of each edge.

Fish base

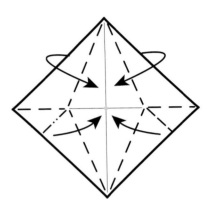

Take a square sheet of paper and position it like a diamond shape. Fold it in half, horizontally, from top to bottom and unfold. Do the same folding vertically. Fold the bottom edges to the central horizontal crease and unfold.

Fold the top edges in the same way and then re-fold the bottom edges while making sure to lift the central folds upwards.

Decorating origami

There are no rules about decorating origami it is an opportunity to try new creative techniques and to express yourself. Don't just colour in each area, think about geometric or 'free' patterns, as well as adding texture. Here are some ideas you could try.

Coloured pencils
These allow you to create complex patterns with fine detail.

Wax crayon
These will give you a rougher result and the colours are often more vibrant.

Felt–tip pen
Again, you will get bright colours but they usually pass through the paper, so these pens are better used to produce patterns rather than filing in large areas.

Glitter

If you carefully apply glue to certain areas of the paper, you can sprinkle glitter on them.

Collage

You could cut up magazines or patterned paper and glue the shapes onto the paper. Scrapbooking paper would work well.

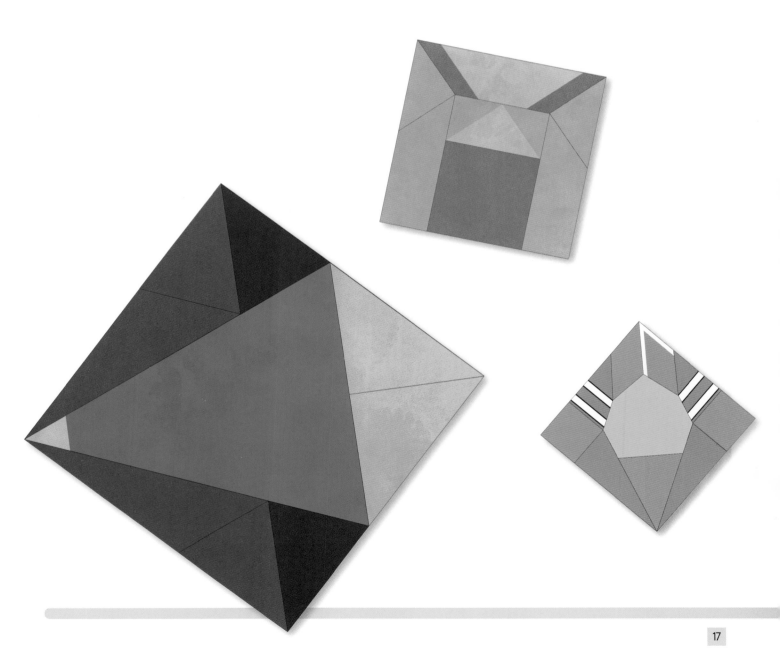

BEGINNER PROJECTS

CROWN

Traditional design

A very easy sequence produces a model that is 2D until the very end, when the model reveals its three-dimensional beauty.

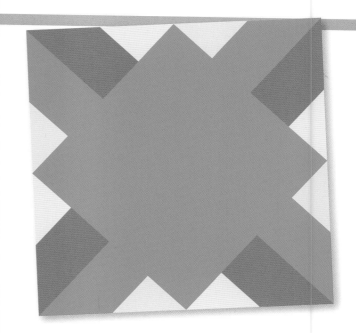

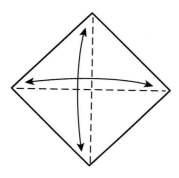

1) Plain side upwards, crease and unfold both diagonals.

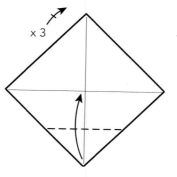

2) Fold a corner to the centre. Repeat 3 times. Turn the paper over.

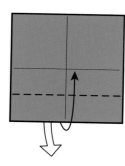

3) Fold the lower edge to the centre, allowing a hidden corner to "flip out".

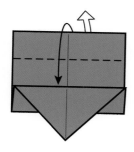

4) Repeat the last step on the upper half.

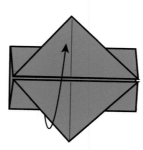

5) Lift up a single layer

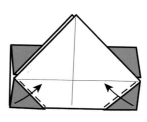

6) Fold the lower corners inwards.

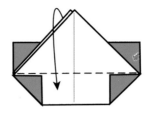

7) Fold down two layers.

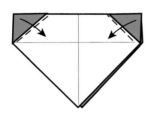

8) Fold in the upper corners.

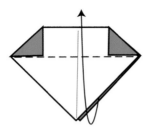

9) Fold a single layer upwards.

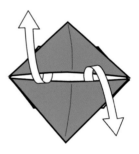

10) Put your fingers inside the pocket and carefully open the model into 3D.

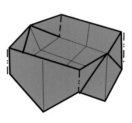

11) Pinch the corners to shape the final model. Turn the paper over.

12) Complete.

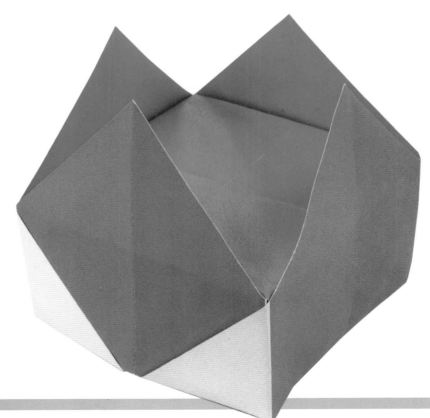

CUP

Traditional design

Amazingly enough, this cup is fully functioning. It's ideal for party snacks or decorations, although it won't hold liquid for more than a minute or so – it is made out of paper afterall!

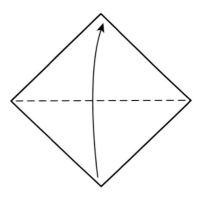

1) Plain side upwards, fold in half from corner to corner.

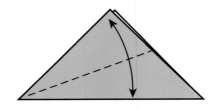

2) Fold the upper left edge to the lower edge, crease and unfold.

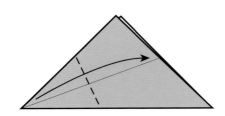

3) Fold the lower left corner to the end of the crease made in the last step.

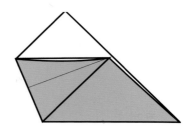

4) This is the result. Turn the paper over.

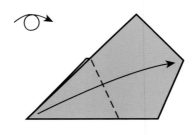

5) Fold the lower left corner to touch the opposite corner.

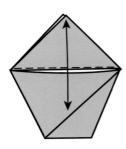

6) Fold the upper triangle down, crease and unfold.

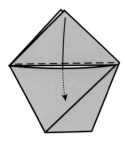

7) Refold the flap down, tucking it into the pocket.

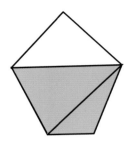

8) This is the result. Turn the paper over.

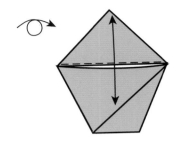

9) Fold the upper triangle down, crease and unfold.

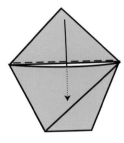

10) Refold the flap down, tucking it into the pocket. Open the pocket at the top a little way.

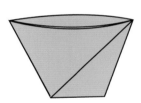

11) Complete.

WHALE

Traditional design

This is one of the simplest designs that use a traditional form known as a Fish base (see page 15). You can alter steps 7 and 9 to create different variations.

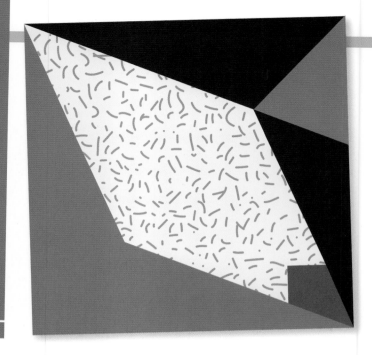

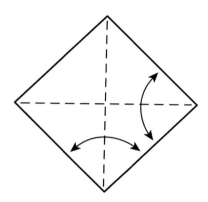

1) Plain side upwards, crease and unfold both diagonals.

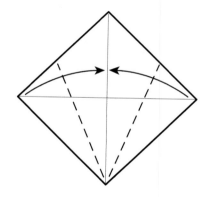

2) Fold the lower edges to the vertical centre crease.

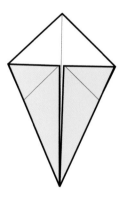

3) This is the result. Turn the paper over.

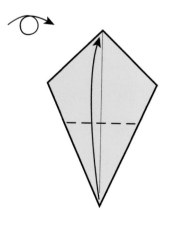

4) Fold the lower corner to the top corner.

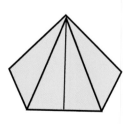

5) This is the result. Turn the paper over.

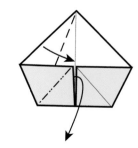

6) Fold the inside coloured corner downwards, at the same time folding the left edge inwards.

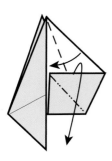

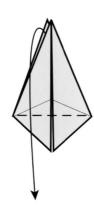

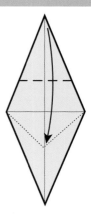

7) This is the result. Repeat on the right side.

8) Fold one of the two flaps downwards.

9) Fold the top corner to (roughly) where the hidden corners are.

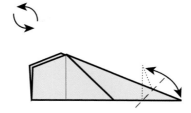

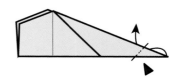

10) Fold in half from left to right. Rotate the paper anti-clockwise.

11) Fold the tail to match the dotted line, crease and unfold.

12) Reverse the tail between the two layers to point upwards.

13) Complete.

BELLFLOWER

Design by David Petty

The folding of the model becomes 3D quite quickly. Take care to hold the paper gently without making any unintentional creases of distortions. You want the final form to be free from surplus creases!

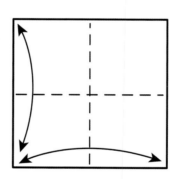

1) Plain side upwards, fold in half, crease and unfold, in both directions.

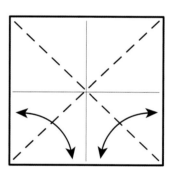

2) Crease and unfold both diagonals. Turn the paper over.

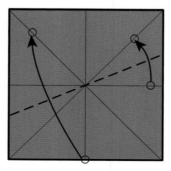

3) Make a crease which passes through the centre of the paper, so that the circled points meet.

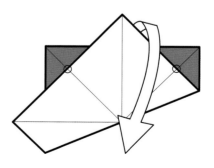

4) Unfold the paper.

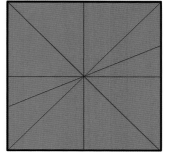 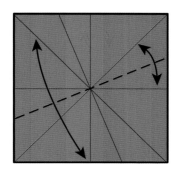

5) This is the result. Rotate the paper 90 degrees clockwise.

6) Repeat step 3. Turn the paper over.

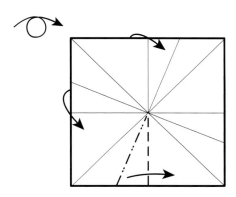
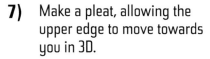
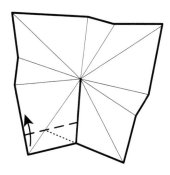

7) Make a pleat, allowing the upper edge to move towards you in 3D.

8) Fold a small flap over.

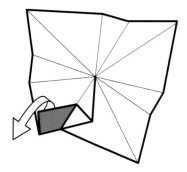
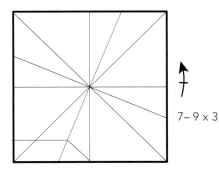

9) This is the result. Unfold again.

10) Repeat steps 7–9 on the three remaining sides.

7–9 x 3

BELLFLOWER CONTINUED

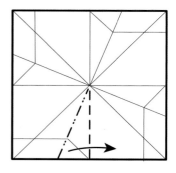

11) Re-form one of the pleats.

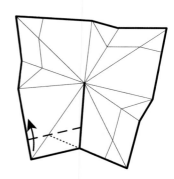

12) Fold the flap upwards.

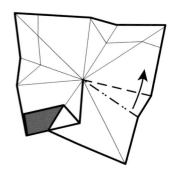

13) Form another pleat.

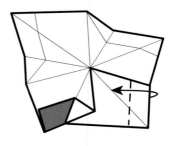

14) Fold another flap in.

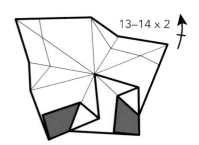

13–14 x 2

15) This is the result. Repeat steps 13-14 on the two remaining sides. Turn the model over.

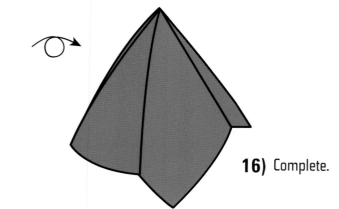

16) Complete.

BUTTONHOLE

Traditional design

This simple design has a surprise ending where the flower blossoms in front of your eyes. Experiment with step 8 to produce different results.

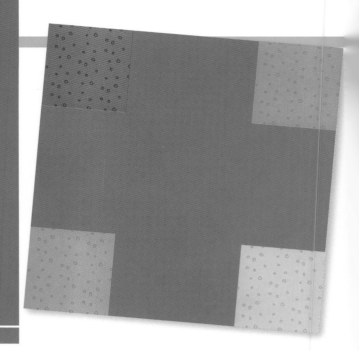

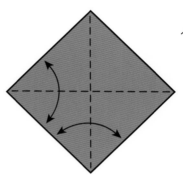

1) Starting with the pattern upwards, crease and unfold both diagonals. Turn the paper over.

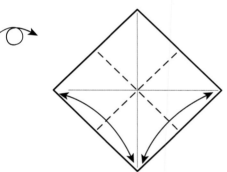

2) Fold in half side to side, crease and unfold, in both directions.

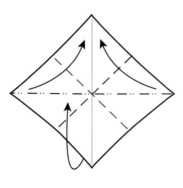

3) Collapse the paper upwards using existing creases.

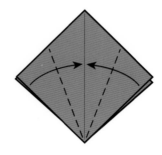

4) Fold two lower edges to the vertical centre. Turn the paper over.

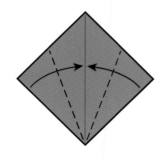

5) Again, fold two lower edges to the vertical centre.

6) Fold a single layer from left to right.

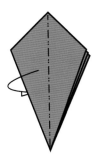

7) Fold a single layer behind on the left.

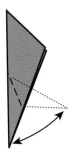

8) Fold the bottom point to the right matching the dotted lines pictured. Unfold again.

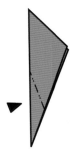

9) Inside reverse fold the same point in between the layers.

10) This is the result. Carefully peel open the layers at the top.

11) Complete.

DOG

Design by Nick Robinson

Here is a simple design that reveals itself at the very end. You can alter the folds from step 6 onwards to create different proportions.

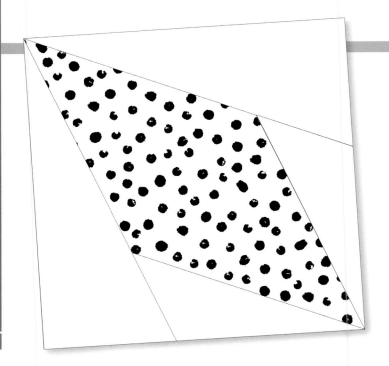

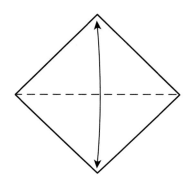

1) Plain side upwards, crease and unfold a diagonal.

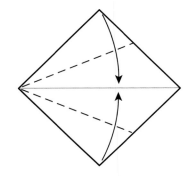

2) Fold both left edges to the horizontal centre.

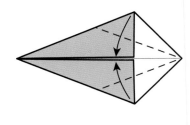

3) Fold the right edges to the horizontal centre. Turn the paper over.

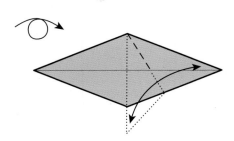

4) Fold so the upper right edge lies on the vertical centre. Crease where shown, then unfold.

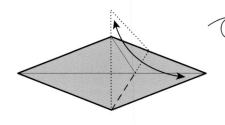

5) Repeat in the opposite direction with the lower right edge. Turn the paper over.

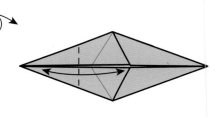

6) Fold the left corner to the inner corners, crease and unfold.

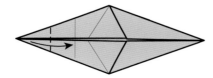

7) Fold the same corner to the recent crease.

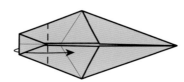

8) Refold on an existing crease.

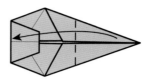

9) Fold the right corner to the opposite end.

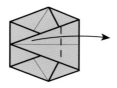

10) Fold the corner back to the left (you can choose how big the tail is here!)

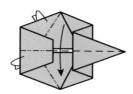

11) Fold the right side in half downwards. At the same time fold the three mountain folds. The model should form itself (with luck!)

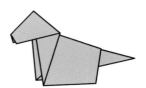

12) Complete.

GLIDER

Traditional design

To launch, the central flap forming the body should be on top. Hold between thumb and forefinger, above your head. Release with a really gentle push forwards. The design will not do acrobatics, but should perform a long, slow glide to the ground.

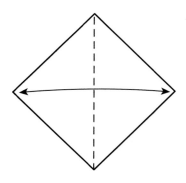

1) Plain side upwards, crease and unfold both diagonals. Turn the paper over.

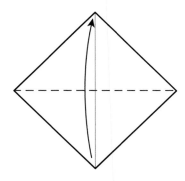

2) Fold in half upwards.

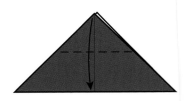

3) Fold both upper corners to the centre of the lower edge.

4) Fold so the circled points meet.

5) Repeat on the right side.

6) This is the result. Turn the paper over.

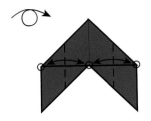

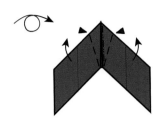

7) Fold the circled corners to the centre, crease and unfold. Turn the paper over.

8) Pinch the centre together, forming the mountain crease and folding the central point to either side to form the valley creases. The outer corners will rotate forwards.

9) Complete.

BLINKING EYE

Design by Nick Robinson

This is an action model – by holding the flaps at the back and moving them in and out, you can make the eye blink. You'll notice that this project requires you to colour or decorate both sides of your design.

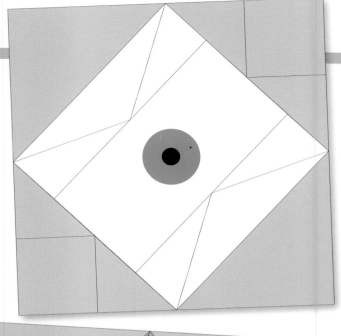

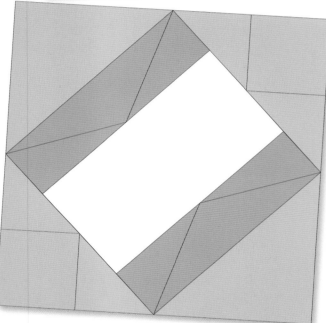

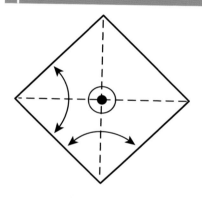

1) With the eye side upwards, crease and unfold both diagonals.

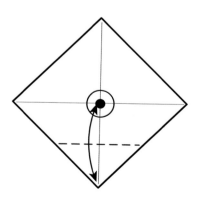

2) Fold the lower corner to the centre, crease and unfold.

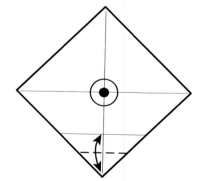

3) Fold the lower corner to the recent crease, crease and unfold.

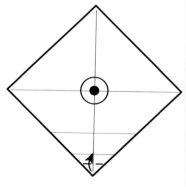

4) Again, fold the corner to the recent crease.

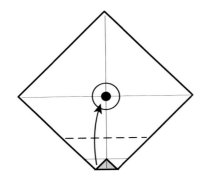
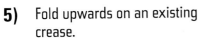

5) Fold upwards on an existing crease.

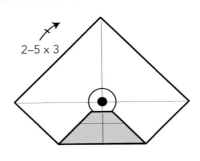

6) Repeat steps 2–5 on the three other corners.

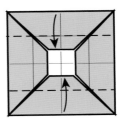

7) Fold the upper and lower corners to the horizontal centre.

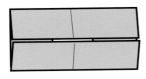

8) This is the result. Turn the paper over.

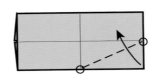

9) Fold the lower right corner between the circled points.

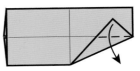

10) Fold the inner corner down along the horizontal centre.

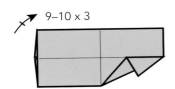

11) Repeat steps 9–10 on the three other corners.

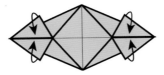

12) Fold the small flaps so they meet each other at 90 degrees to the model. These are handles to make the eye blink.

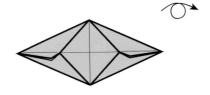

13) Turn the design around.

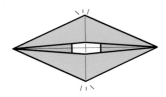

14) Complete.

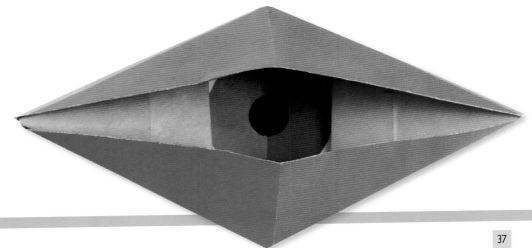

SNAPPER

Traditional design

This is a fun "action" model which you can use to pick up and "swallow" small objects. Can you catch a real fly?

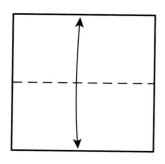

1) Plain side upwards, crease in half and unfold.

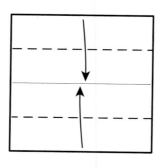

2) Fold upper and lower edges to the centre crease.

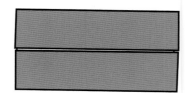

3) This is the result. Turn the paper over.

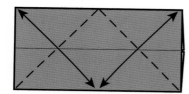

4) Fold both upper corners to lie on the lower edge, crease and unfold.

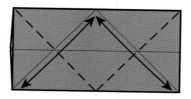

5) Fold both lower corners to lie on the upper edge, crease and unfold.

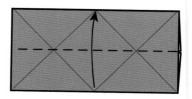

6) Fold in half upwards.

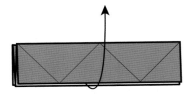

7) Unfold a single layer.

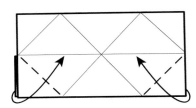

8) Fold all layers at the lower corners inwards.

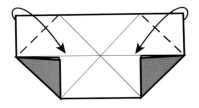

9) Fold the upper corners inwards as well.

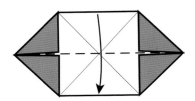

10) Fold in half downwards.

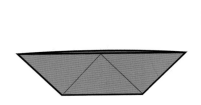

11) This is the result. Rotate the model.

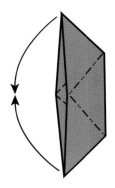

12) Open the layers slightly and fold upper and lower corners to meet.

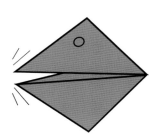

13) Complete.

CHAIR

Traditional design

This model is part of a series of designs that all follow the same initial folding sequence. If you want to invent your own variation, you can try going freeform after step 8!

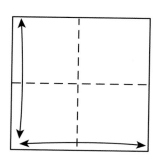

1) Plain side upwards, fold in half, crease and unfold, in both directions.

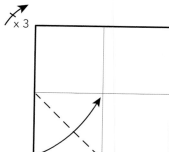

2) Fold a corner to the centre. Repeat with the three other corners.

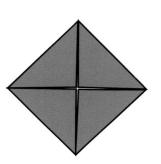

3) This is the result. Turn the paper over.

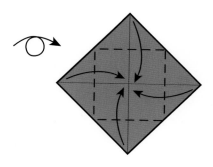

4) Once again, fold all four corners to the centre.

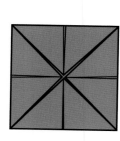

5) This is the result. Turn the paper over.

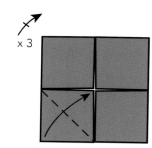

6) Once again, fold all four corners to the centre!

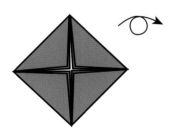

7) This is the result. Turn the paper over.

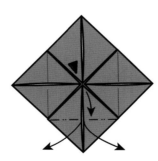

8) Fold a corner down from the centre, carefully opening the paper out on either side and pressing flat.

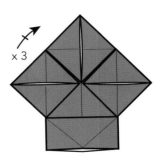

9) This is the result. Repeat three times.

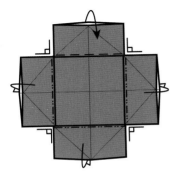

10) Fold three flaps down at right angle. Fold the last flap up at right angles!

11) Complete.

WOLF

Design by Nick Robinson

Here is another design that begins with the Fish base (see page 15). This simple starting point has a lot of creative potential, as you can see from the other designs in this book that use it (Whale on page 24 and Tropical Fish on page 74). Hold by the two rear corners and move them apart to open the jaws.

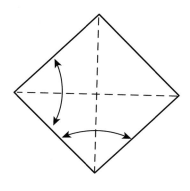

1) Pain side upwards, crease and unfold both diagonals.

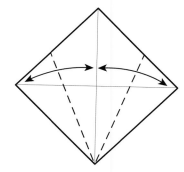

2) Fold the lower edges to the centre, crease where shown, then unfold.

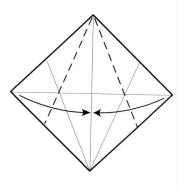

3) Fold the upper edges to the centre.

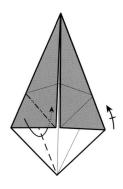

4) Refold on the lower valley crease, wrapping the paper inside. Repeat on the right.

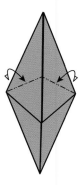

5) You can see two creases near the centre. Fold the paper behind, crease and unfold so that the creases are both mountain creases. Turn the paper over.

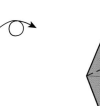

6) Fold the lower edges to meet behind. At the same time, pinch the upper flap into a point – see the next drawing.

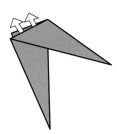

7) Fold up the two hidden points.

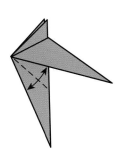

8) Fold the lower edge to the horizontal edge. Crease and unfold.

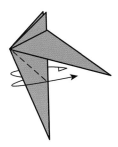

9) Open the back of the paper slightly, then wrap each side of the lower flap to the outside.

10) Complete.

FISH PROFILE

Design by Rob Snyder

This is an unusual approach to origami as you are creating a kind of silhouette, especially fun if you hold it up to the sun. You can create many variations by altering the steps 7 and beyond.

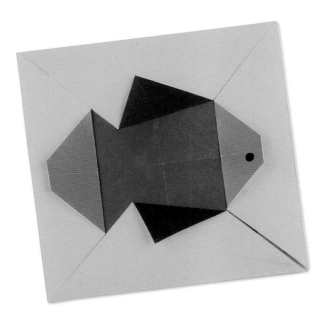

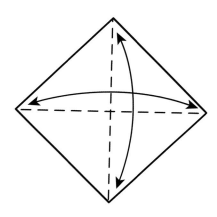

1) Plain side upwards, crease and unfold both diagonals.

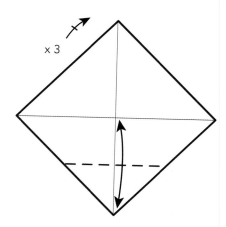

2) Fold a corner to the centre, crease and unfold. Repeat three times.

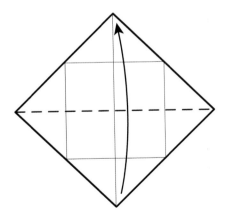

3) Fold in half upwards.

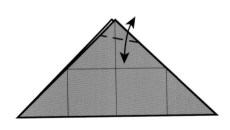

4) Make a slightly offset crease through both layers then unfold.

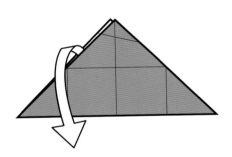

5) Open out the paper fully.

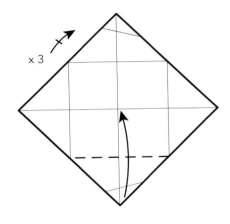

6) Refold all corners to the centre.

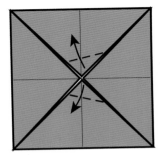

7) Fold out two flaps using existing creases.

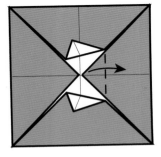

8) Fold an inner corner to the right, starting at the plain side corners.

FISH PROFILE CONTINUED

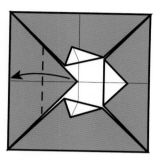

9) Fold an inner corner to the centre of the left edge.

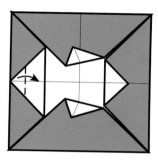

10) Fold the corner back in a little way.

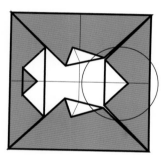

11) This is the result. Now we focus on the circled area.

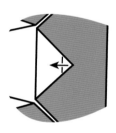

12) Fold over a tiny corner.

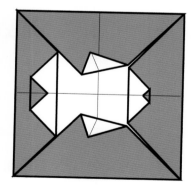

13) Complete.

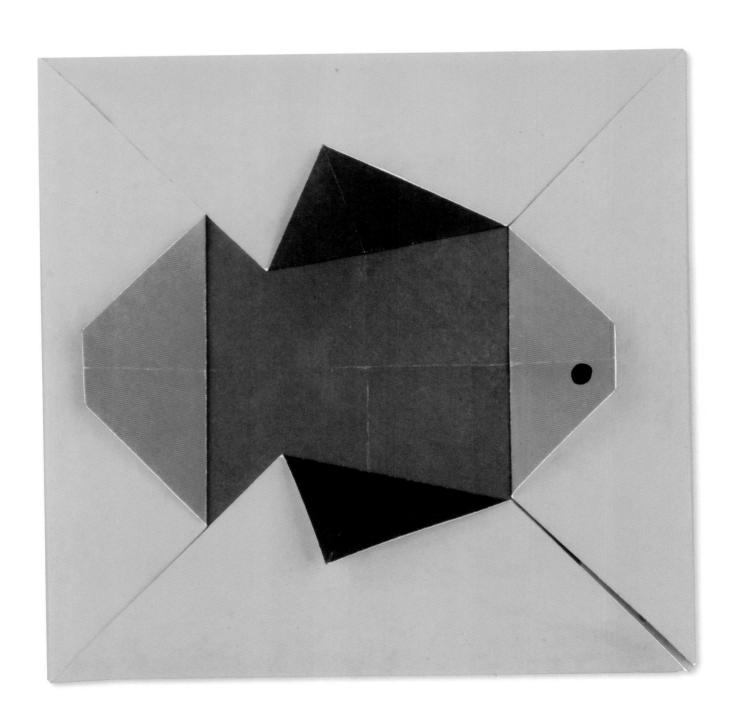

ADVANCED PROJECTS

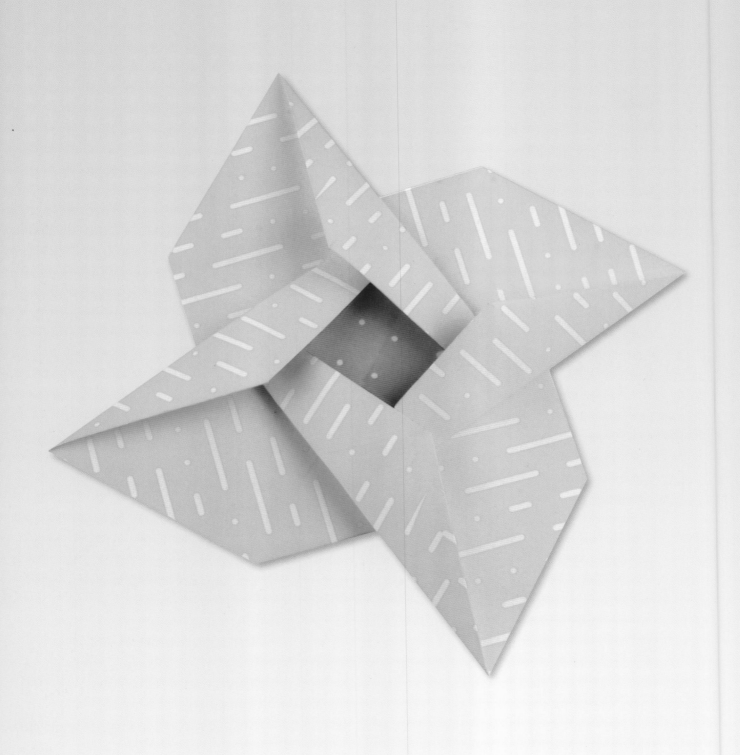

ELEPHANT HEAD

Design by Nick Robinson

Every crease in this model has an easy location. You can stop at step 11 for the simplest version, or carry on to further shape the ears and create a stand at the back.

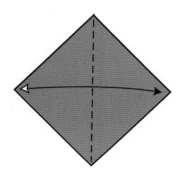

1) White side down, crease and unfold a vertical diagonal.

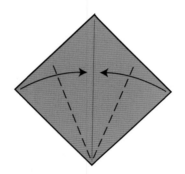

2) Fold the lower edges to the middle.

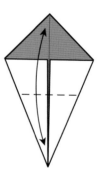

3) Crease in half from bottom to top.

4) Unfold the flaps and turn the paper over.

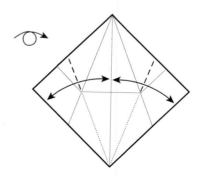

5) Make folds similar to step 2, but on the crease where shown.

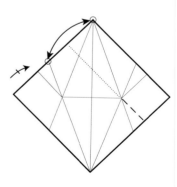

6) Fold so the circled points meet, on the crease where shown. Repeat on the other side.

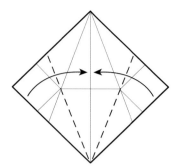

7) Refold the flaps inwards.

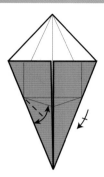

8) Fold an outer edge to the nearest crease, creasing only where shown. Unfold and repeat on the right.

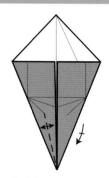

9) Fold an outer edge to the middle crease, creasing only where shown. Unfold and repeat on the right.

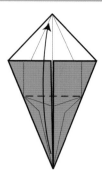

10) Fold in half upwards. Rotate the paper 180 degrees.

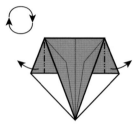

11) Ease out the ears – no new creases needed.

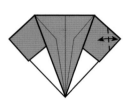

12) Make small pre-creases on both sides. The exact location isn't important. Turn the paper over.

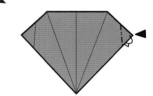

13) Reverse the corners between the layers on both sides.

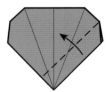

14) On the right, fold the layers over.

15) Make a similar fold on the left side.

16) Fold the flap up, crease and unfold. This forms a stand for the model. Turn the paper over.

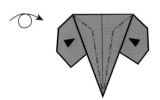

17) Gently reinforce these creases so the head becomes 3D.

18) Complete.

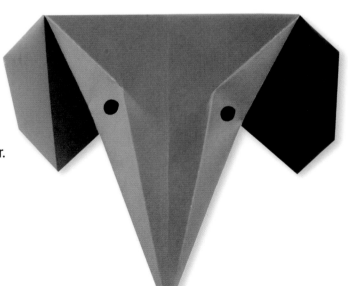

CONTAINER

Design by Nick Robinson

A practical design, this makes a perfect container for pens and pencils! Remember to make all creases carefully and accurately.

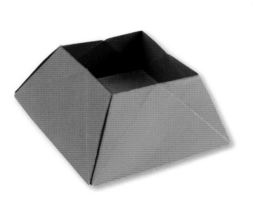

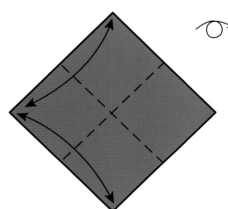

1) Patterned side upwards, fold in half, crease and unfold, in both directions. Turn the paper over.

2) Fold a corner to the middle. Repeat three times.

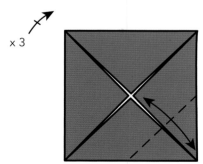

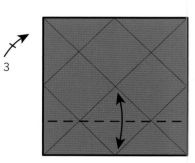

3) Fold a corner to the middle. Repeat three times. Turn the paper over.

4) Fold the lower edge to the middle. Repeat three times.

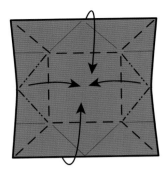

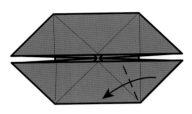

5) Fold using only these (existing) creases.

6) This is the result. Fold the lower right edge to lie along the bottom edge . . .

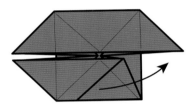

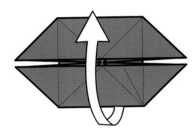

7) . . .like this. Crease firmly then unfold.

8) Open out a hidden corner and unfold it fully.

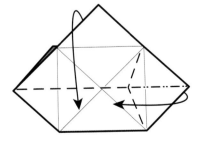

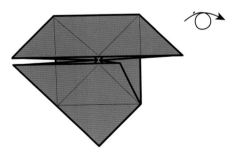

9) Fold the flap down again, making a reverse fold on the right.

10) This is the result. Turn the paper over.

CONTAINER CONTINUED

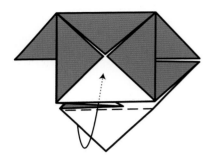

11) Fold the flap up, tucking it into a pocket above the reversed flap inside.

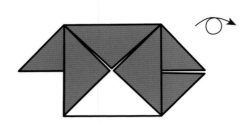

12) This will "lock" that side together. Turn the paper over.

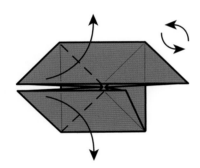

13) Fold the two flaps on the left in opposite directions and rotate the paper anti-clockwise.

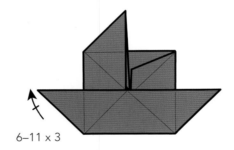

6–11 x 3

14) Repeat steps 6-11 three more times. The final time, you have less paper to work with.

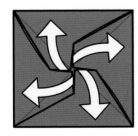

15) Carefully open the sides outwards and form into 3D. sharpen all the edges.

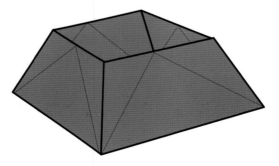

16) Complete.

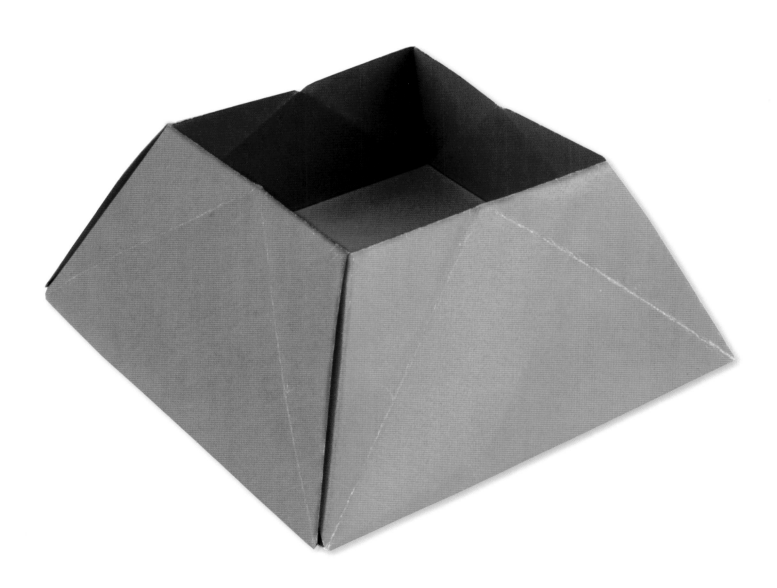

DUCK

Design by Tony O'Hare

Duck is a wonderful design where the main creases are all perfectly located to produce a stylized model of great beauty.

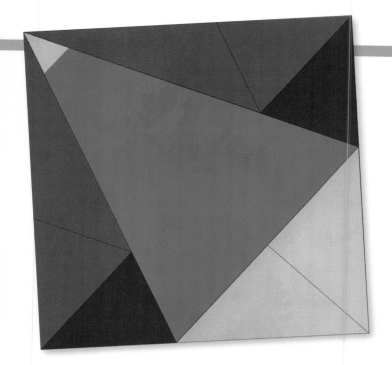

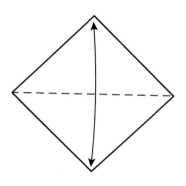

1) Crease and unfold a horizontal diagonal.

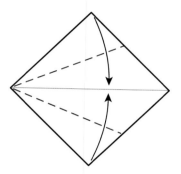

2) Fold two edges to the middle crease.

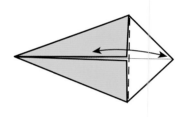

3) Fold the plain section triangle to the left, crease and unfold. Turn the paper over.

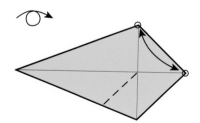

4) Fold so two corners meet, crease where shown, then unfold.

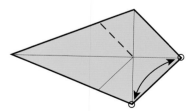

5) Repeat in the other direction.

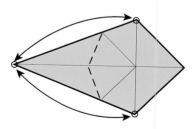

6) Fold the left corner to the other circled corners, creasing only where shown, then unfolding.

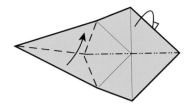

7) Fold the upper right edge behind, at the same time folding the flap on the left in half.

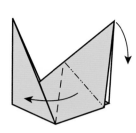

8) Use these creases (on both sides) to swivel the right side to the left.

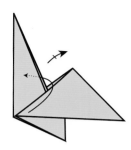

9) Tuck the triangular flap inside layers of the "neck". Repeat on the other side.

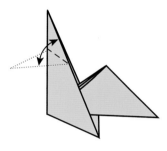

10) Fold the point to match the dotted line, crease and unfold.

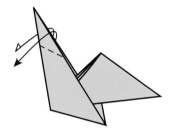

11) Wrap the layers around the outside using the crease made in the last step.

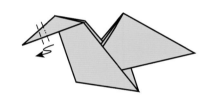

12) Fold the beak in and out again.

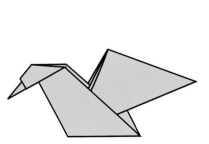

13) Complete.

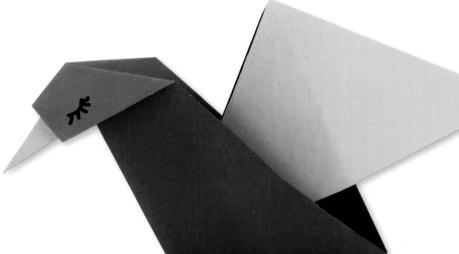

MONKEY

Design by Kunihiko Kasahara

A cute representation of the subject, created by a Japanese master of origami. You can vary the poses by making small adjustments to the folding sequence.

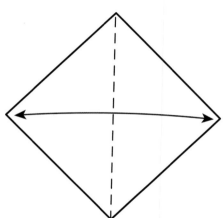

1) Plain side upwards, crease and unfold a diagonal.

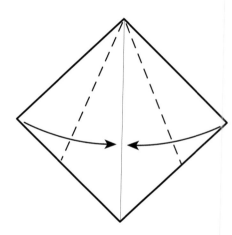

2) Fold both upper edges to the horizontal crease.

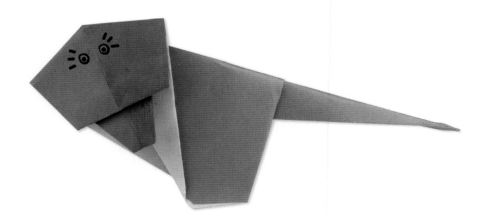

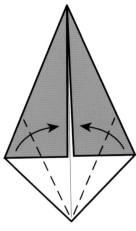

3) Fold the lower edges to the middle.

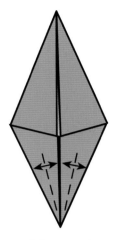

4) Fold each lower edge to the middle, creasing more or less where shown.

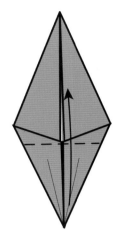

5) Fold the lower half upwards where shown.

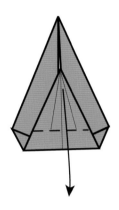

6) Fold the flap back down.

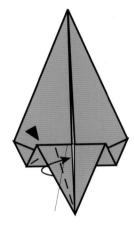

7) Refold on an existing crease, carefully squashing the paper flat at the top.

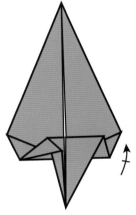

8) This is the result. Repeat on the right side.

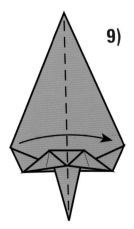

9) Fold in half from left to right. Rotate the paper slightly.

10) Fold the top corner to the bottom corner, crease and unfold.

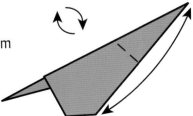

MONKEY CONTINUED

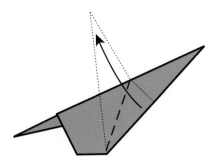

11) Fold to match the dotted line.

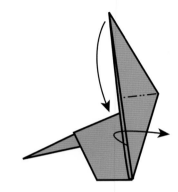

12) Open out a single layer and fold the top corner down.

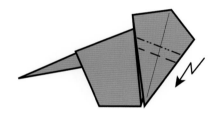

13) Make a pleat on the head.

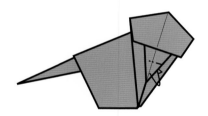

14) Fold the tip behind.

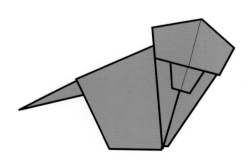

15) Complete.

PAJARITA

Traditional design

This model has been used for more than 100 years in Spain. Today, it appears on the logo for the Spanish Paperfolding Association (AEP). This folding sequence is particularly pleasing, so you can enjoy making it again and again!

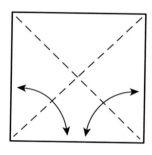

1) Plain side upwards, crease and unfold both diagonals.

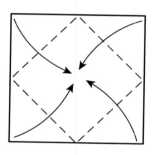

2) Fold all corners to the middle.

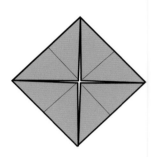

3) This is the result. Turn the paper over.

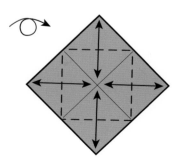

4) Fold all corners to the middle, crease and unfold.

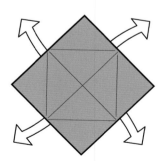

5) Unfold back to a square and turn the paper over.

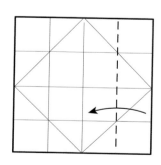

6) Fold the right edge in.

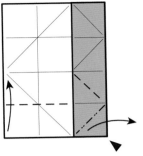

7) Lift up the lower corner and form a point as you fold up the lower edge.

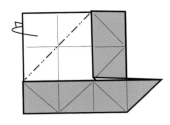

8) Fold a corner behind.

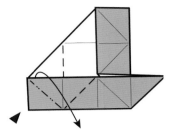

9) Another move like step 7.

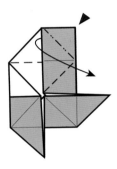

10) And another.

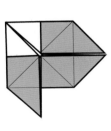

11) This is the result. Turn the paper over.

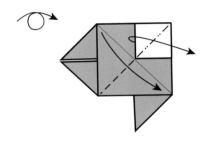

12) Fold the top left corner to the bottom right, opening out a plain side flap as you do so.

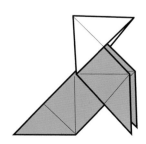

13) Complete.

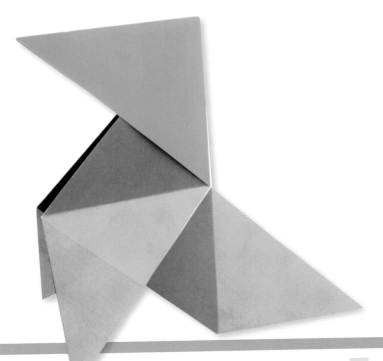

RABBIT

Design by Suzanna Krikskovics

This talented designer from Hungary has made many simple yet elegant designs. This one is a a rewarding design to make that requires a little patience and careful attention to detail.

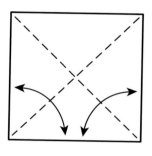

1) Plain side upwards, crease and unfold both diagonals. Turn the paper over.

2) Fold two corners to the middle, crease and unfold. Turn the paper over.

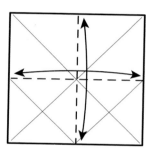

3) Fold in half in both directions, crease and unfold.

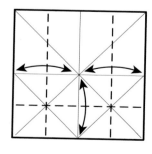

4) Fold three edges to the middle, crease and unfold.

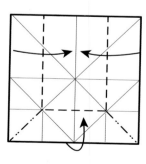

5) Fold three sides in, forming points at the lower corners.

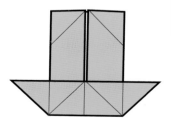

6) This is the result. Turn the paper over.

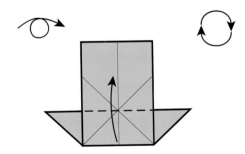

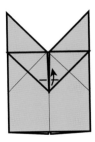

7) Fold the lower edge upwards. Rotate the paper.

8) Fold the two flaps upwards.

9) Fold a small flap upwards. Turn the paper over.

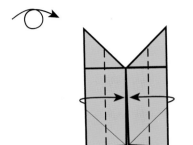

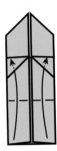

10) Fold the vertical edges to the middle.

11) Fold the lower edge to a horizontal folded edge, crease and unfold.

12) Refold the flap, tucking it into two pockets. Turn the paper over.

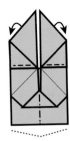

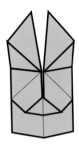

13) Fold the ears slightly forwards and make the paper slightly 3D so it will stand up.

14) Complete.

ROCKING PENGUIN

Design by Rob Snyder

There are many origami penguins, but very few that actually move! This clever design forms a penguin that will rock back and forth.

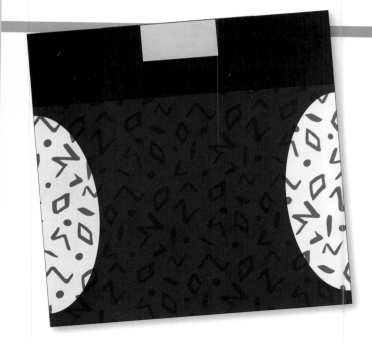

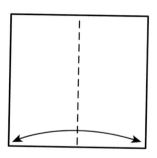

1) Plain side upwards, crease in half and unfold.

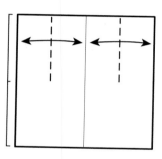

2) Add quarter creases in the upper half of the paper.

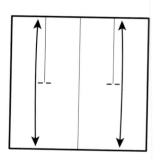

3) Fold in half upwards, but pinch only on the quarter creases.

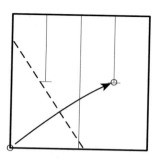

4) Fold the bottom left corner to the circled pinchmark.

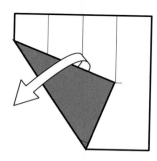

5) This is the result. Unfold.

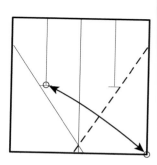

6) Repeat on the lower right corner.

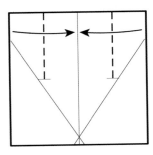

7) Fold in on the quarter creases – do not extend these creases!

8) Fold the upper corners inwards.

9) Fold the triangular flap downwards.

10) Fold the tips of the corners behind.

11) Fold the inner corner to the top, crease and unfold half way to form the beak.

12) Complete.

SHUBUNKIN

Design by Rob Snyder

This design allows for some beautiful decoration on the tail fins. Remember that not all creases have to be made firmly. Why not try to make the tail creases more gently?

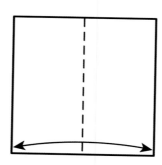

1) Plain side upwards, crease in half and unfold.

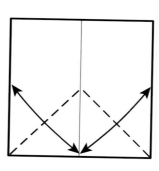

2) Make two diagonal creases that reach as far as the vertical middle crease.

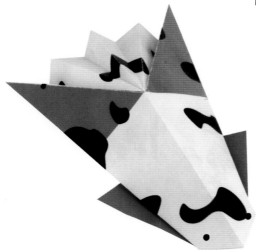

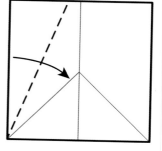

3) Fold the left edge to lie on the diagonal crease.

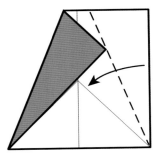

4) Repeat on the right side.

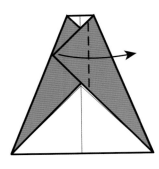

5) Fold a corner out just to the right of the vertical middle crease.

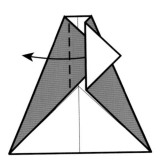

6) Repeat on the left.

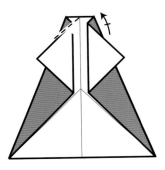

7) Fold the upper left and right corners inwards.

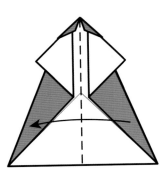

8) Fold in half from right to left.

9) Fold the lower right edge to lie on the crease.

SHUBUNKIN CONTINUED

10) Fold the triangular flap in half, crease and unfold. Unfold to step 9.

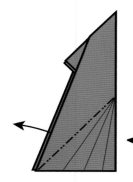

11) Reverse fold the flap inside on the innermost crease.

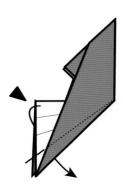

12) Reverse the flap back out on the next crease.

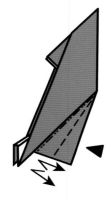

13) Reverse the flap in and out again on the remaining creases. Rotate the model anti-clockwise.

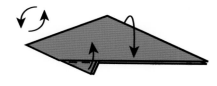

14) Fold the lower fins out at 90 degrees. Open out the tail fins.

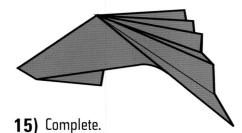

15) Complete.

TULIP

Traditional design

This model is quite unusual in that it is 2D until the final steps, when you inflate it to become 3D. You may need to fold it several times to perfect the folding sequence!

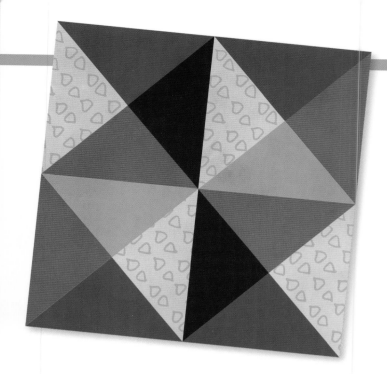

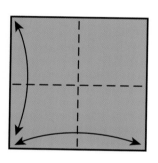

1) White side down, fold in half, crease and unfold, in both directions. Turn the paper over.

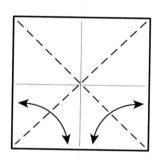

2) Crease and unfold both diagonals.

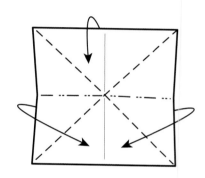

3) Use these existing folds to collapse the paper downwards.

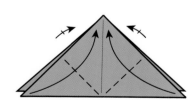

4) Fold two corners to the top corner. Repeat on the other side.

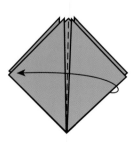

5) Fold a single flap from right to left. Turn the paper over.

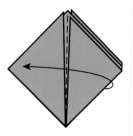

6) Fold a single flap from right to left.

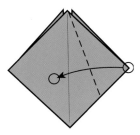

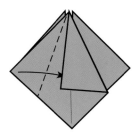

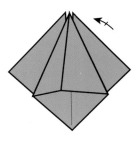

7) Fold the right corner to the circled point.

8) Fold the left corner over and tuck it inside the pocket of the other flap. You may need to adjust both flaps to get a snug fit.

9) This is the result. Repeat on the other side.

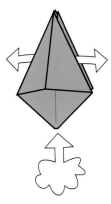

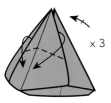

× 3

10) Blow sharply into the hole at the bottom and allow the paper to inflate. Don't let it open too much!

11) Carefully wrap a flap downwards. Repeat with the other flaps.

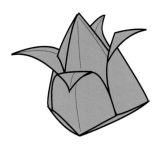

12) Complete.

TROPICAL FISH

Design by Chris Alexander

This design begins with a Fish base (see page 15). From that point, some clever moves are made to create an elegant tropical fish.

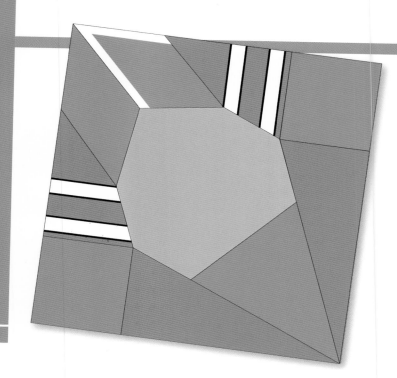

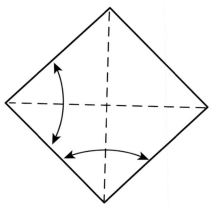

1) Plain side upwards, crease and unfold both diagonals.

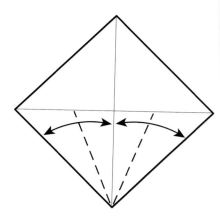

2) Fold the lower edges to the middle, crease where shown, then unfold.

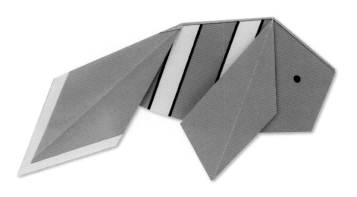

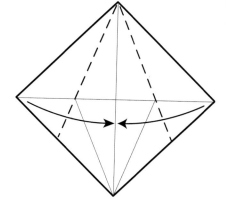

3) Fold the upper edges to the middle.

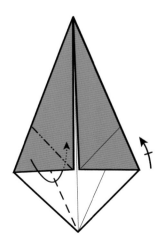

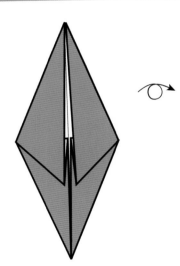

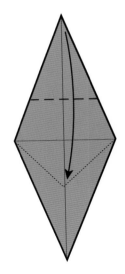

4) Refold on the lower valley crease, wrapping the paper inside. Repeat on the right.

5) This is the result. Turn the paper over.

6) Fold the top corner down to match the hidden corners underneath.

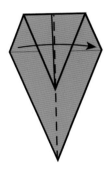

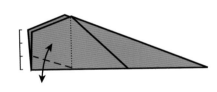

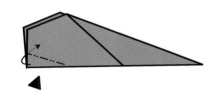

7) Fold in half from left to right. Rotate the paper.

8) Fold a corner upwards where shown, crease and unfold.

9) Push the corner inside.

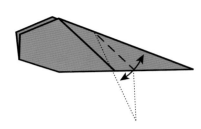

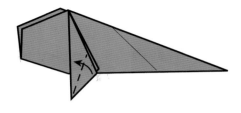

10) Fold the sharp flap to match the dotted line, crease and unfold.

11) Fold a flap to lie on the dotted line, crease and unfold.

12) Squash open the flap.

TROPICAL FISH CONTINUED

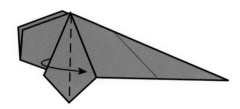

13) Fold the flap in half.

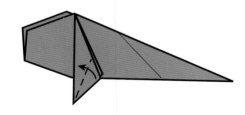

14) Fold the lower edge to the vertical edge.

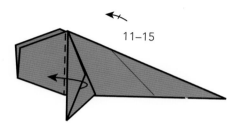

11–15

15) Fold the narrow flap to the left. Repeat steps 11–15 on the other side.

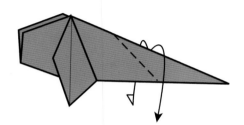

16) Open the tail slightly and wrap a layer of the tail to either side.

17) Ease out a layer from inside the tail and fold it to the right.

18) Fold half of the tail to the left.

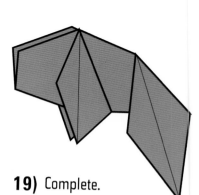

19) Complete.

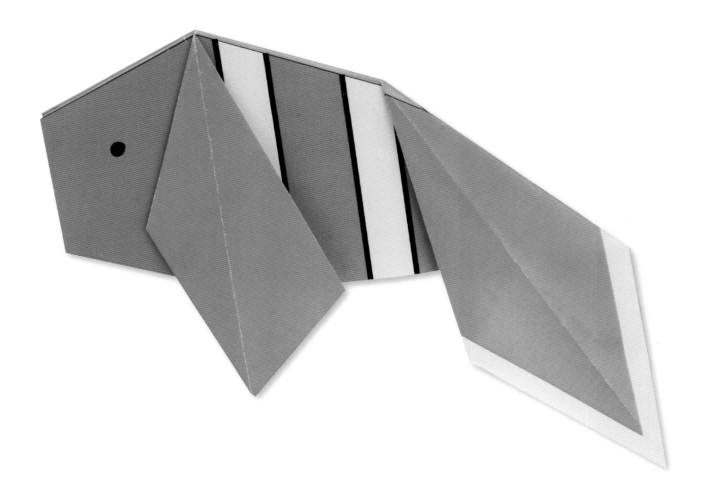

SPACE SHUTTLE

Design by Nick Robinson

Although it is not a flying model, this design looks great if you hang it from a thread. Several creases need to be inverted or reversed, so make all creases sharply.

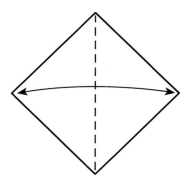

1) Plain side upwards, crease and unfold a diagonal.

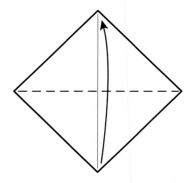

2) Fold in half upwards.

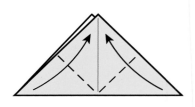

3) Fold the two lower corners to the top corner.

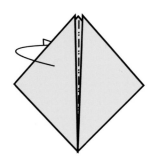

4) Fold the left half behind.

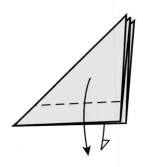

5) Fold one flap down on either side.

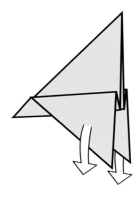

6) Pull the flaps fully down.

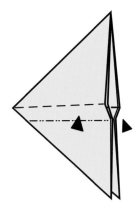

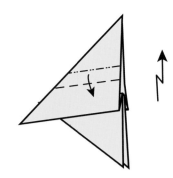

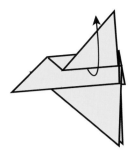

7) Swap the creases around to refold both flaps into the model.

8) Make a pleat through all layers.

9) Unfold the pleat.

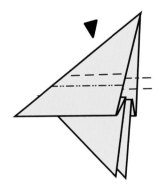

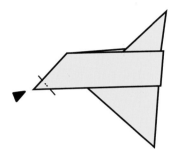

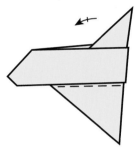

10) Reverse fold the top flap in and out of the model.

11) Fold the tip of the nose inside.

12) Fold both wings out at right angles.

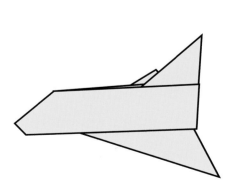

13) Complete.

HEN

Design by Tony O'Hare

By altering angles at steps 5, 7 and 9, you can create many variations on the basic design. Why not create a whole family of chickens?

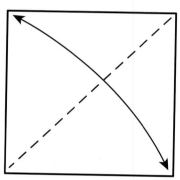

1) Plain side upwards, crease and unfold a diagonal.

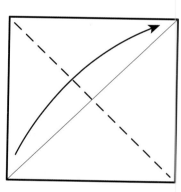

2) Fold corner to corner in the other direction.

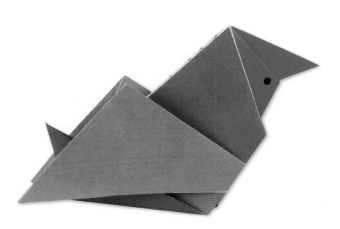

3) Fold two corners to the right-angled corner.

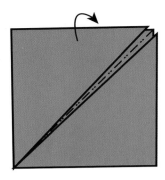

4) Fold the upper half behind.

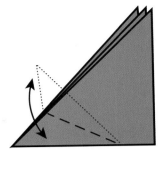

5) Fold to match the dotted line, crease and unfold.

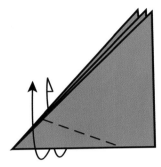

6) Open the layers and wrap one to either side on the recent crease.

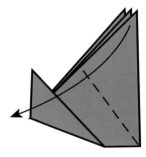

7) Fold one flap down – see the next drawing for the exact position.

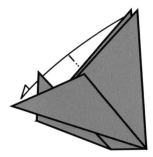

8) Repeat on the rear flap.

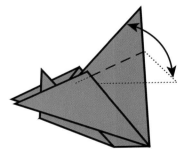

9) Fold the top corner to match the dotted line, crease and unfold.

HEN CONTINUED

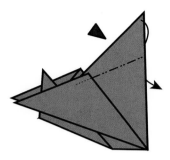

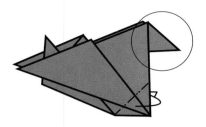

10) Push the top flap inside on the recent creases.

11) Fold two corners in at the lower right. Next we focus on the circled area.

12) Fold the small flap in half, crease and unfold.

13) Open the layers and wrap one layer to the outside, on both sides.

14) Complete.

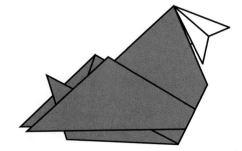

HIGH HEELS

Design by Nick Robinson

This is a chance to make some origami fashion items! The final step may need slight adjustments to make the shoe stand up. Obviously you'll need to make a pair.

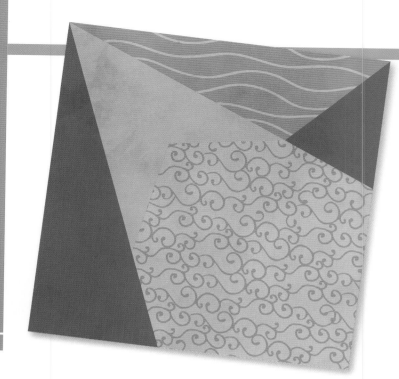

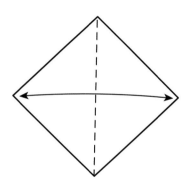

1) Plain side upwards, crease and unfold a diagonal.

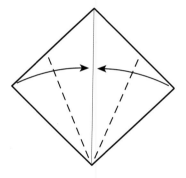

2) Fold the lower edges to the middle crease.

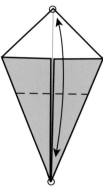

3) Fold in half from bottom to top, crease and unfold.

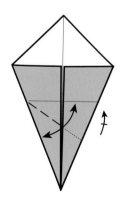

4) Fold the lower left edge to the horizontal crease, creasing only where shown, then unfolding. Repeat in the other direction.

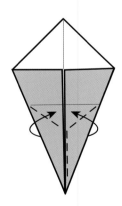

5) Fold both lower edges in at the same time, pressing together to form a point. The model is 3D at this point.

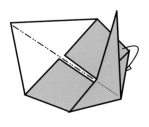

6) Fold the right half behind.

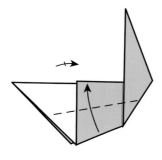

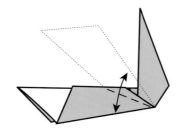

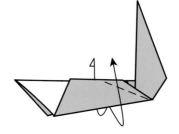

7) Fold the bottom edge to the horizontal edge, crease and unfold. Repeat on the other side.

8) Fold all the lower paper to match the dotted line, crease firmly and unfold.

9) Wrap each side of the lower layers around to the outside.

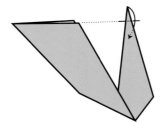

10) Fold the sharp point inside to line up with the dotted line, so it can stand up! Turn the paper around.

11) Complete.

STAR

Design by Nick Robinson

This is a purely decorative design, based around a twisting fold first discovered by Shuzo Fujimoto. There are many possibilities for creating other types of stars in this way.

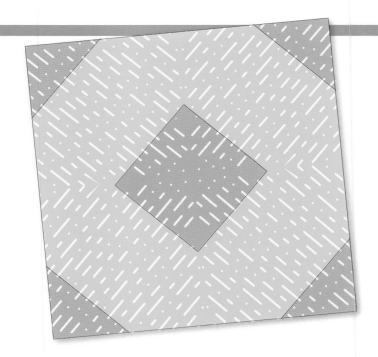

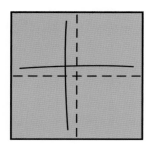

1) Start with the white side down. Fold in half, crease and unfold in both directions.

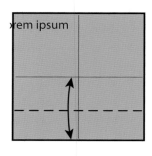

2) Fold each edge to the middle, crease and unfold. Turn the paper over.

3) Fold a corner to the nearest creases. Repeat 3 times.

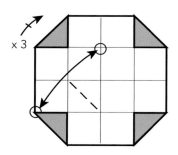

4) Fold so the circled points meet, but crease only where shown. Repeat 3 times.

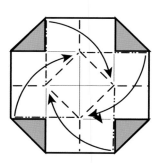

5) Start to form these creases and gently twist the paper clockwise.

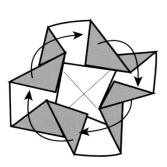

6) This is how the folds should look in progress.

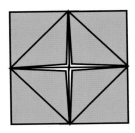

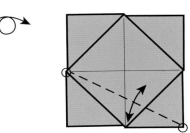

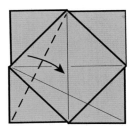

7) This is the result. Turn the paper over.

8) Fold between the circled points. Crease and unfold.

9) Fold in the top left corner in the same way.

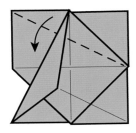

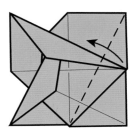

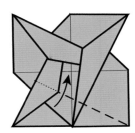

10) Fold the top left section in.

11) And the right hand side, as shown.

12) Finally, refold on an existing crease, reversing the crease along the dotted line so it is the same as the others.

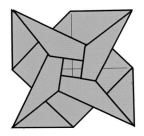

13) Complete.

ACKWORTH DISH

Design by Nick Robinson

When folding dishes or containers, it's best to use as few creases as possible, so the end result is pure and simple. The model was named after a small village where it was created.

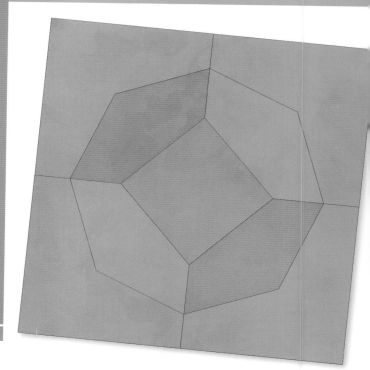

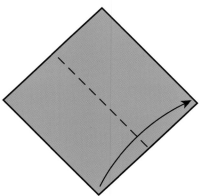

1) Start with the pattern upwards. Fold in half, side to opposite side.

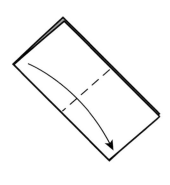

2) Fold in half again.

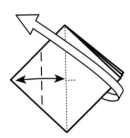

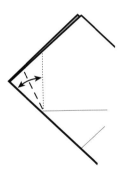

3) Fold the left corner to the approximate middle of the paper, crease and unfold, then unfold step 2.

4) (Enlarged view) Fold to an imaginary vertical line, crease and unfold.

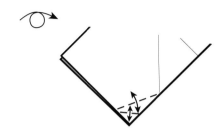

5) Fold a small part of the upper edge to touch the recent crease, then unfold. Turn the paper over side to side.

6) Repeat the last two steps on this side.

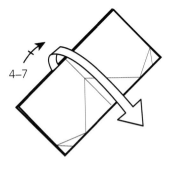

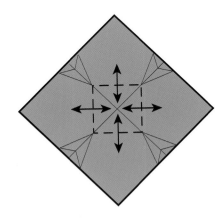

7) Unfold back to a square, then fold one half in the other direction and repeat steps 4–7 before opening fully again.

8) Make sure these creases are all valley folds. Turn the paper over.

ACKWORTH DISH CONTINUED

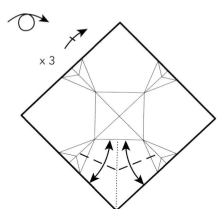

9) Fold a lower edge to lie on the horizontal crease. Do not crease past the middle of the paper. Repeat on the opposite side.

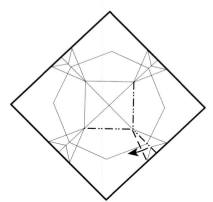

10) Make the mountain folds so the sides fold downwards slightly and the paper becomes 3D. Then pleat the paper using existing creases.

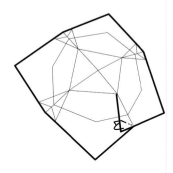

11) Fold the corner behind, again using existing creases.

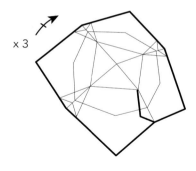

12) This is the result. Repeat the last two steps on the other three sides.

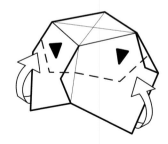

13) Carefully wrap the outer edges around using existing creases. Fold carefully! Finally, turn the model over.

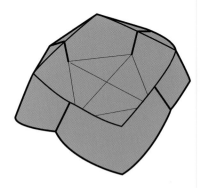

14) Complete.

ANGEL

Design by Nick Robinson

This is perhaps the most complex design in the book, so fold slowly and carefully and be prepared to make it several times before it starts to look elegant.

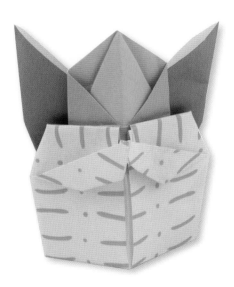

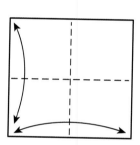

1) Plain side upwards, fold in half, crease and unfold, in both directions.

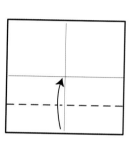

2) Fold the lower edge to the middle.

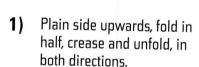

3) Fold the left and right edges to the vertical middle.

4) Fold the internal corners to the outer edges.

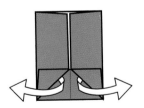

5) Carefully ease out the paper and flatten it.

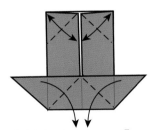

6) Fold the two lower flaps down. Crease and unfold at the top.

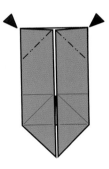

7) Push/reverse the upper corners inside.

8) Fold the lower left flap to the right.

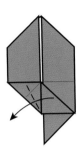

9) Fold the flap back, so that a crease lines up with an edge beneath it.

10) Fold the outer corner in.

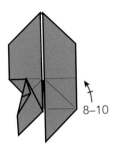

11) Repeat steps 8–10 on the right side.

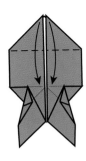

12) Fold two corners down at the top. Turn the paper over.

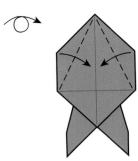

13) Fold the sides in between the corners.

ANGEL CONTINUED

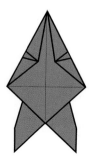

14) This is the result. Turn the paper over.

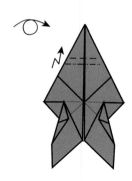

15) Pleat the flap near the top.

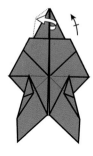

16) On the left, ease out some paper to form the head. Repeat on the right.

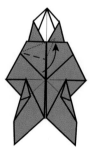

17) Fold a flap over to meet the dotted line.

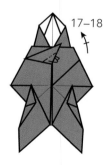

18) Fold a corner behind to shape the arm. Repeat steps 17–18 on the right side.

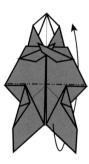

19) Fold the lower half of the model behind.

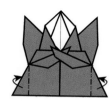

20) Fold the sides behind.

21) Fold in half behind.

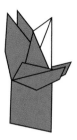

22) Complete.

Acknowledgements

Nick Robinson would like to thank his wife, Ali, and children Nick Jnr. and Daisy for their love and support; Moggies Rhubarb and Pickle for chewing the designs; and Joan and Xiǎoxián (congratulations!). Additionally, all his many origami friends throughout the world and all at Arcturus Publishing for their input and patience with this project.

Thanks to the designers featured in this book for sharing their work. The models were created as follows. Tropical fish – Chris Alexander; Bellflower – David Petty; Monkey – Kunihiko Kasahara; Space Shuttle, Container, Eye, High Heel Shoe, Wolf, Ackworth Dish, Elephant Head, Dog, Star and Angel – Nick Robinson; Rocking Penguin, Fish profile and Shubunkin – Rob Snyder; Duck and Hen – Tony O'Hare; and Rabbit – Zsuzsanna Kricskovics. The remaining designs are traditional. In origami, there is always scope for new, independent variations, but every effort has been made to identify the original/earliest creator of any design that has inspired these projects.

Nicks plays and loves Fender guitars and his websites are www.origami.me.uk and www.looping.me.uk.